MINDFULNESS JOURNAL FOR PARENTS

Mindfulness Journal for Parents

Prompts and Practices to Stay Calm, Present, and Connected

Josephine Atluri

ROCKRIDGE PRESS

For general information on our other products and services or to obtain technical support, please contact our Customer Care Department within the United States at (866) 744-2665, or outside the United States at (510) 253-0500.

Rockridge Press publishes its books in a variety of electronic and print formats. Some content that appears in print may not be available in electronic books, and vice versa.

TRADEMARKS: Rockridge Press and the Rockridge Press logo are trademarks or registered trademarks of Callisto Media Inc. and/or its affiliates, in the United States and other countries, and may not be used without written permission. All other trademarks are the property of their respective owners. Rockridge Press is not associated with any product or vendor mentioned in this book.

Interior and Cover Designer: Michael Cook
Art Producer: Sara Feinstein
Editor: Mo Mozuch

Illustrations used under license from iStock.com.

ISBN: Print 978-1-64876-469-1

R0

To my mother, Carol,
forever mindful of your everlasting presence
in my heart. PJMMDD—My heart beats for you.

Contents

Introduction: Why Mindful Parenting

It was one of those Monday mornings where we were rushing to do everything on time. We were almost out the door when my three-year-old suddenly burst into tears after spilling his drink. Then, my 10-year-old began a frantic, last-minute search for homework. I was on the verge of succumbing to the swirl of chaos as the stress sent me toward a meltdown.

I paused. I took several slow, deep breaths. The noise around me softened. The breathing technique instantly reduced my stress. Thus, I was more effective and useful in my response to my kids. This translated into a drama-free homework search while I carried my son in my arms to comfort him. I was calm amid the chaos.

In spite of our best efforts as parents, we constantly find ourselves navigating stressful situations with our children against the backdrop of an overwhelmingly busy life. Every day we hope to do better as parents because we love our children. Yet, in order to flourish as caregivers, we need the framework and tools to manage this stress. Awareness is very important, because understanding ourselves enhances our ability to empathize and build deeper, more connected relationships.

An awareness of oneself and the present moment, without judgment, is the essence of mindful parenting. Being mindful affords us the opportunity to gently witness life as it unfolds without worrying about the past or the future. We can then direct our mindful awareness to our bodies, our emotions, our surroundings, and our children.

Mindful parenting gives you the tools to develop a meaningful relationship with your child based on a foundation of conscious compassion. No matter what type of parenting style you prefer, mindfulness provides a scaffolding that makes other parenting techniques more effective. Mindfulness facilitates greater understanding of your child's true nature apart from the expectations placed upon them.

When I discovered how to practice mindfulness and began coaching parents, it was a game changer. Suddenly, life became more manageable and fulfilling even as it became more complex raising five kids ranging in ages from 5 to 14. I have helped thousands of parents cultivate their own awareness and connect with their authentic self to forge more vibrant relationships with their children. The practices and exercises found in this journal are similar to strategies I have used with many clients and discussed in my podcast, *Responding to Life: Talking Health, Fertility, and Parenthood.*

Crafted for the busy but well-intentioned caregiver, this journal is an approachable guided mindfulness journey. This book won't erase the problems that you will face in parenthood, but it will allow you to respond to these challenges in a calmer, more purposeful way. When building new habits, one way to ensure success is by pairing your mindfulness practice with an existing ritual, such as when you first wake up and brush your teeth or right before you go to bed. All you need is a few minutes a day to reap the benefits of mindfulness, such as reduced stress and anxiety, increased focus and productivity, enhanced emotional awareness and positivity, and improvements in health and relationships.

On this journey to mindfulness, you will:

· Understand the critical role of mindfulness in parenting through fellow parents' stories.
· Reflect on and journal your experiences via prompts meant to evoke self-discovery and reawaken awareness.
· Practice a variety of mindfulness exercises to add to your self-care repertoire.
· Transform your approach to yourself and parenthood.

These activities are meant to give you quick moments of self-reflection and mindfulness so you can thrive in parenthood rather than just surviving it.

Regaining Your Focus

Practicing the activities in this section will awaken your consciousness and cultivate your awareness of yourself, others, and your environment. This will translate into how you care for yourself and how you care for your children. When you infuse mindfulness into your parenting, you evolve into a more present and understanding parent and enrich your relationship with your child.

Multitasking Mistake

Juggling a family, work, and home life can feel so overwhelming, it seems that multitasking is the only way to stay above water. However, splitting your attention can be counterproductive. While Michael was busy working, he was also talking to his five-year-old son, Terrance. Michael tuned out the conversation and unknowingly agreed to Terrance's request. Later, Michael's wife asked him, "Did you tell Terrance we'd buy him a new bike?" Michael couldn't recall the conversation with his son. He felt awful for getting so caught up in work and for needing to break the news to Terrance that they would not be buying him a new bike. While enticing, multitasking prevents awareness of the present moment. Focusing on one thing at a time, however, gets the job done in a mindful, productive way.

You Are Your Parents

Often our innate parenting habits stem from our childhood experiences. Part of being mindful in the present moment is understanding the root of our actions and emotions. Think of when you did something worthy of praise when you were a kid. What happened? What happened when you made a mistake? What was the response from your caregivers in each instance?

_____

_____

_____

_____

_____

_____

_____

_____

_____

_____

_____

_____

_____

Parenting Wins

When starting a new journey, it's important to understand the impetus and purpose of your endeavor. With that in mind, what is working well with your parenting style? Describe your parenting wins. What are your parenting areas of growth? Exploring your parenting approach is a first step toward being mindful.

_____

_____

_____

_____

_____

_____

_____

_____

_____

_____

_____

_____

Watch in Wonder

We often operate on autopilot when it comes to parenting. In life's chaos, we forget to experience the joy of parenting and to witness the happiness of our children. The next time your child is playing, simply watch them from afar. Observe their emotions and see if you can vicariously experience their unadulterated joy. If you find your mind wandering during this practice, acknowledge the thought and know that you can return to it later. Then go back to witnessing your child's genuine bliss.

Great Expectations

What are your expectations of this journey for yourself and for your relationship with your child? Do your best to frame your statements in a positive way. Reflect on what you wrote and see if there are any expectations that stem from ideals that others imposed on you as you grew up. Do these expectations still align with your current personal beliefs and parenting values?

Developing Intentions

Set an intention for your day as well as an overall intention for this journal. An intention is the purpose or motivation behind the actions you take to achieve a goal. Think of them as gentle reminders or a road map for how you want your day to unfold. Example of intentions are: being more grateful, opening up to possibility, embracing love. What is your intention today? Why? How does it connect with your intention for this journal?

Emotional Awareness

Mindfulness is our ability to witness the present moment as it unfolds before us in relation to both physical things, such as our bodies and our environment, and intangible things, such as our emotions. Reflect on your day. Make a list of the different emotions you experienced. Describe what happened or any triggers you may have encountered to make these feelings surface. When being mindful of your feelings, remember to incorporate self-kindness into whatever you experience and be free of judgment.

Get in Tune

A great way to start being mindful is to tune in to your senses. Write down what you're experiencing in this moment with each of the five senses (hearing, touch, smell, sight, and taste) and expand on your descriptions as much as possible. Throughout today and perhaps the rest of your week, see if you can tune in to these senses. Record those observations here.

_____

_____

_____

_____

_____

_____

_____

_____

_____

_____

_____

_____

_____

Listen to Your Body

Another way to practice mindfulness is to explore how your body feels in the moment. How did you wake up this morning? How did your body adapt and move throughout the day? Make a note here about any areas of tightness, stress, or pain. Were you able to do anything to alleviate the tension? Notice during the rest of the week if you have the same or different areas of tension and if there are certain stretches or adjustments that you can do to relieve any tightness.

Breathing Break

The next time you feel overwhelmed or distracted, try this quick breathing exercise to bring mindfulness into your day and shift into a state of calm awareness.

1. For four seconds each: Breathe in slowly. Hold your breath. Breathe out. Hold your breath.

2. You can either repeat this pattern as many times as you need to feel calm and mindful or simply do it once for a total of 16 seconds of present-moment awareness.

A Strong Start

Starting your morning in a mindful way sets the tone for your day, and ending your day mindfully offers a chance for focused reflection. Read and answer the following prompt when you wake up and then again before bed: Observe and write down everything around you—things you may see, hear, smell, or feel. Are these things you take for granted?

Witnessing Flow

Witnessing the breath is a great introduction to mindfulness. Try this daily for a week at the beginning or end of your day to feel connected and calm.

1. Sit or lie down. Close your eyes.

2. Take a slow, deep breath in through your nose. Exhale slowly out of your mouth.

3. Continue this pattern as you notice the rise and fall of your body with every inhalation and exhalation.

4. Witness the flow of your breath, staying focused on the rhythm of your body.

5. Practice for three to five minutes, then open your eyes.

Finding Joy

Journal about a recent moment when you experienced joy. Reflect on whether that feeling of joy spread to other parts of your day. If your joy was interrupted, explore what happened. Why did it have the power to pause or disrupt your happiness?

_____

_____

_____

_____

_____

_____

_____

_____

_____

_____

_____

_____

Autopilot Paused

For parents with never-ending to-do lists, accomplishing tasks feels like it should take precedence over playing with our kids. One evening, Tanya was running on autopilot getting dinner ready while also preparing lunch boxes. In the midst of her flow, Tanya's seven-year-old daughter, Marigold, demanded attention. Tanya redirected Marigold to play with her blocks, but a few minutes later, Marigold returned crying. Tanya hit the pause button on her tasks and together they calmly solved Marigold's problem. Marigold cherished the five uninterrupted minutes with her mom. While it can feel like there's never enough time to do everything, a few minutes of undivided, mindful attention can make a world of difference to our children, positively impacting their emotional well-being.

Self-Care Strategies

Pick a time in the next day or two and plan a deliberate mini-break where you do something for yourself, then journal about the experience. What will you do? How did it feel taking that break: good, selfish, unwarranted, necessary? Create a list of other self-care strategies you could do in planned moments of your day or as in-the-moment stress-management techniques.

Pause for Presence

Go for a 15-minute stroll outside by yourself without any devices. Look at your surroundings. Use your five senses in your observations. Notice sounds, textures, colors, the feel of the air, and the smell of the environment. If you find your mind wandering, gently acknowledge your thought with compassion and without judgment and return your focus to your environment.

Mindfulness Barriers

What do you think prevents you from being mindful at various times in your day? Make a list of these things. Identifying mindfulness barriers enhances awareness and empowers you to find ways to break them down.

Giving Yourself a Break

Cultivating mindfulness helps us look inward to observe how we feel and how we treat ourselves. This awareness can nurture acceptance, improve self-worth, and develop one's love of self. Practicing self-compassion and kindness leads to greater joy and peace within yourself and in your relationships with your child or children.

Progress, Not Perfection

Striving toward perfection can create unnecessary stress. What standards do you hold yourself to? What standards do you think others hold you to? Circle the ones where you can make progress without the pressure of perfection. Cross out ideals that feel impossible or don't align with your values and purpose in life.

Self-Imposed Standards   **Standards Others Held You To**

Limiting Beliefs

We all have beliefs about ourselves and the world that limit us, beliefs such as, "I am not smart enough." They prevent us from moving forward. Think of a story you tell yourself that puts limits on you. Write it down. Then challenge these beliefs with a sentence or two that provides evidence that the story isn't true.

_____

_____

_____

_____

_____

_____

_____

_____

_____

_____

_____

Boost Your Self-Confidence

Our brains are wired to look for something wrong. It's part of our natural instinct to protect ourselves from danger. This negativity bias, however, often gets directed at oneself. Here's a great way to practice a mindset shift from negativity to positivity: Make a list of everything you are really good at doing. Which ones come naturally, and which ones required a lot of hard work? Describe a moment where you did something exceptional. The next time you feel a diminished sense of self-worth, review this list for a boost of self-confidence.

You Are Not Your Thoughts

A key to mindfulness is accepting that you will have both positive and negative thoughts. With the thousands of thoughts we think daily, however, it's hard not to be influenced by these negative thoughts. Write down any thoughts that you had yesterday or today about yourself, good or bad, as a practice in observing and acknowledging your thoughts. How did these thoughts feel? How did they affect your day?

Labeling Your Thoughts

One way to increase self-awareness is to label our thoughts. This promotes detachment and reminds us that we are not defined by our thoughts. For the purpose of this exercise, start with these five basic labels: planning, feeling, sensation/sound, remembering, and criticizing.

1. Select a point of focus, such as your breath or an object in your room.

2. Sit in silence and just observe your focal point.

3. When a thought occurs, label it with one of the five basic labels.

4. Return to your point of focus and repeat this process as needed for three to five minutes.

5. Afterward, write down any new labels that you can use in the future based on the types of thoughts you had.

Be Kind to Yourself

Do you treat yourself the way you treat people you care about? Brainstorm ways you can be kind to yourself, picking one for each day of the week. It might help to think of how you would care for others and use these same ideas on yourself. Always remember that self-love and self-care are essential, not selfish, and make you a better parent.

You're Doing Great, Mama!

Parents often fall into the trap of comparison, which causes insecurity and robs us of our joy. On Halloween, Yolanda volunteered at a party in her son's first-grade classroom. Seeing the elaborate snacks others brought made her feel terrible about her simple treats. Yolanda's inner critic began the usual tirade of negativity. Just then her son ran to her, hugged her tight, and said, "I'm so happy you're here, Mama!" Yolanda met the moment with joyful presence and shifted her inner voice to say, "You're doing great, mama!" She saw herself through the perspective of her loving son, not her inner critic. In times of self-doubt, one way to shift from a state of negativity to positivity is to challenge your inner critic by practicing self-love and compassion.

Drop the Negative Labels

Throughout life we pick up labels: hard worker, super mom, planner. Unknowingly, we define ourselves by these labels, and they then guide our choices. List the labels you've had throughout life. Cross out any outdated or negative ones and circle the positive ones that are left. This self-encouragement practice helps you realize your potential as a person and a parent.

Quieting the Inner Critic

Think of something your inner critic said to you in the last few days that you didn't challenge or correct. Write it down, then write what you should have said in response. Use this technique to challenge that inner critic by showing yourself support and love instead.

Shout-Out to Myself

Write down some compliments that you have received over the course of your life that made you happy and think differently about yourself. Then write down five compliments you can give yourself today.

_____

_____

_____

_____

_____

_____

_____

_____

_____

_____

_____

_____

I Am

Affirmations are phrases that offer strength, support, confidence, and love to oneself. They are phrases such as "I am brave," "I am resilient," and "I am enough." Affirmations are great tools to use when you feel discouraged because they disrupt negative patterns with positivity. Make a list of "I am" affirmations. Use it the next time you feel down and need encouragement.

Self-Love Exercise

1. Look over your list of affirmations and select one to be your mantra or point of focus.

2. Close your eyes. Notice your breath.

3. Inhale and say the affirmation to yourself. Gently repeat this phrase throughout your meditation.

4. If a thought occurs, acknowledge, label, and release it. Return to your affirmation.

5. Try to do this for five minutes.

The Good, the Bad, the Ugly

We all have moments as parents that we regret or feel guilty about. Part of conscious awareness is accepting and not judging both the good and the bad. Take this opportunity to let one of these moments out on paper without any judgment. Acknowledge your feelings and consider the root causes for why you felt this.

_____

_____

_____

_____

_____

_____

_____

_____

_____

_____

_____

Shame on You. It's Okay.

Shame gets a bad rap but can actually be healthy. It lets you check in with yourself. "Are you sure you want to say that? Or do that?" Shame becomes counterproductive when it's unkind and debasing without providing room for growth. Reflect on a time when you experienced healthy and unhealthy shame. What happened after each of those moments?

A Letter to Your Younger Self

Recall a moment from your childhood when you experienced emotional pain, felt insecure, or failed at something. Be vulnerable to every aspect of that memory. Now, write a letter to that younger version of yourself in which you offer words of reassurance and kindness. Approach this practice of self-compassion gently. It takes courage to walk through the pain, but it will highlight what you care about and perhaps what you can give yourself permission to release.

_____

_____

_____

_____

_____

_____

_____

_____

_____

_____

_____

_____

_____

_____

Managing Stress and Anxiety

Exploring the sources of your stress and employing the strategies in this section will empower you with the tools to navigate the challenges in your life. Using the science of how our brains work, you will create and strengthen the pathways in your brain to easily access your connection to awareness and calm. Training your brain to manage stress and anxiety will ultimately improve your parent-child relationship.

Fight or Flight

Seemingly harmless things, even if we're not in physical danger, can induce a fight-or-flight response. For instance, one morning Kai read an upsetting email and then saw some news headlines that further provoked him. Unbeknownst to him, he was already in fight-or-flight mode when he sat down for breakfast with his partner, Jackson. Not realizing Kai's disposition, Jackson reminded him of an after-school event that evening. Frustrated and overwhelmed, Kai snapped at his partner, escalating into a fight about schedules and priorities. Had Kai been aware of his triggers and feelings, he could have prevented an outburst. Responding to stressful situations in a mindful way can lead to more positive interactions and outcomes.

Identifying Triggers

A key step to managing stress and anxiety is to recognize how it manifests. Awareness moves us toward making change. Use the chart below to fill in details about one stressful moment or anxious thought each day this week. Understanding your triggers can help you prevent them from happening or know how to better respond to them. Once you've finished, write down any observations that you have about your triggers and brainstorm solutions to countering them.

DAY OF THE WEEK	STRESSFUL MOMENT/ ANXIOUS THOUGHT	WHAT TRIGGERED IT?	OTHER FACTORS (HUNGRY, TIRED, RUNNING LATE, ETC.)
MONDAY			
TUESDAY			
WEDNESDAY			
THURSDAY			
FRIDAY			
SATURDAY			
SUNDAY			

_____

_____

Just Say No

In today's overload culture, we are inundated by stressful situations that trigger our fight-or-flight response. Write about a stressful moment that could have been avoided if you had just said no to something or someone. How did it make you feel saying yes when you didn't want to? Now think of the many ways that you can say no in the future to preserve your mental and emotional well-being.

Breathe It Out

When we are experiencing heightened emotions, our breath is our gateway to instantly shift from the sympathetic nervous system's response of fight or flight to the parasympathetic nervous system's response of rest and digest. The next time you feel triggered by stress, inhale through your nose slowly while keeping count of time. When you exhale through your nose, double the time it took you to inhale. Repeat this process until you start to feel calmer.

Know What You Can Control

Worrying about things that we cannot control breeds anxiety. To diminish unnecessary stress, make a list of things as a parent that you can manage and things that you cannot control. There is a freedom in acknowledging and releasing the things outside of our control. The next time you encounter a challenging situation, ask yourself if it is actually something you can manage.

Emotional Self-Regulation

Write about your last disagreement with your child. What feelings got stirred up? Why? Can you witness these emotions without getting entangled in them and let them go? If it's hard to release, think big picture: Is this disagreement worth the mental energy? Try this technique in the moment during your next stressful interaction.

Prioritize You

What gets in the way of your happiness: obligations, guilt, people? Write about a time when you prioritized others over your well-being and then a time when you took care of yourself first. How did each experience feel? Journal some ways that you can prioritize your happiness.

_____

_____

_____

_____

_____

_____

_____

_____

_____

_____

_____

_____

Shoulda Coulda Woulda

You should do this. You should be that. Expectations spark anxiety and overwhelm. Write a list of 5 to 10 "should statements" you've told yourself. Which of these can you cross off so that you can live life more authentically? For the statements that remain, reframe them to say "I get to do . . ." or "I would like to . . ."

Activating Calm

Upon detecting any type of danger or stressful situation, your body exhibits physical symptoms that alert you of your heightened state. When Belinda brought up homework expectations to her daughter, Lacey, their discussion escalated into an argument. Belinda's heart raced, and her body got hot and shaky. Belinda wanted to scream in frustration at Lacey's defiance. Rather than spiraling into negativity, Belinda tuned in to how she was feeling, realizing she was in a triggered state. While Lacey voiced her opinions, Belinda practiced a breathing technique that slowed her racing heart and cooled her body. This dose of calm deactivated the fight-or-flight response, enabling Belinda to peacefully brainstorm solutions with Lacey. Recognizing your body's response to stress affords the opportunity to interrupt the moment with a calming strategy.

Stress in the Body

When our lives feel threatened in stressful situations, many of our systems—digestive, immune, cardiovascular—react so we can prioritize the parts of our body that will protect us from danger. When you feel stressed, do you notice what's happening in your body? Think about a time when you felt overwhelmed and write down exactly what that stress felt like physically. Do this prompt again in a few days and notice any patterns or differences in how stress manifests in your body.

Body Scan

Body scans are great tools for checking in with your body and releasing tension via meditation.

1. Close your eyes. Slow your breath.

2. Working up your body, check in with your feet, legs, belly, chest, back, hands, arms, shoulders, neck, and then your head (jaw, corners of eyes, brows, forehead)

3. Notice in each section if you feel tension. Breathe into that spot and feel your inhale push out the tightness.

4. Exhale, blowing the tension out of your body.

5. Repeat for each section of your body.

Get Some Z's

Sleep is a great way to curb the onset of stress and anxiety. It refreshes our brain, making it easier to handle the hard stuff. When we are sleep-deprived, we have less tolerance for minor annoyances. Record your current sleep routine for the next week by filling out the chart below. Evaluate your results, then make a list of strategies you can employ to revamp your sleep, such as turning off screens an hour before bed, listening to music, using essential oils, or trying meditation breathing techniques to relax.

DAY OF THE WEEK	ACTIVITIES BEFORE BED	FEELING BEFORE BED (TIRED, ANXIOUS, WIRED, ETC.)	TIME YOU GOT INTO BED AND TIME YOU WOKE UP	FEELING WHEN YOU WOKE UP
MONDAY				
TUESDAY				
WEDNESDAY				
THURSDAY				
FRIDAY				
SATURDAY				
SUNDAY				

Self-Care Tool Kit

It's essential to have a broad range of strategies to help you cope with stress based on your mood. To create your tool kit, grab a piece of paper and write out a list of things that boost your mental, emotional, and/or physical well-being, such as working out, meditating, saying affirmations, or reading a book. Put this list in an actual bag to keep at home, work, or in the car. Add items in the bag necessary for each remedy. Having a mental checklist is good, but a physical kit you can reach for immediately can prevent you from forgetting your options and falling into a rut.

Identifying Fears

Our fears stem from past experiences or from the uncertainty of the future. Mindfulness keeps us in the present to prevent this stress. Write down your parenting fears. What past experiences or future worries dictate your family rules? Now write a factual statement challenging the validity of each fear.

_____

_____

_____

_____

_____

_____

_____

_____

_____

_____

_____

_____

_____

Asking for Help Is a Sign of Strength

In today's society, independence is a source of strength and asking for help can be seen as a sign of weakness. Yet, reducing stress sometimes requires delegation of our tasks. By reframing help as delegation, we infuse it with power and control. What things in your life actually need your full attention? What are things that other people can do for you at home and at work?

Staying Cool When Emotions Run Hot

It's crucial to arm yourself with the knowledge and tools to be less reactive the next time you have a conflict, or when your child has a meltdown. Emotions cloud judgment and stifle positive responses. Mindfulness forges the resilience and compassion that allow you to manage your anger, keep cool during disputes, and maintain healthy relationships.

Parenting Remorse

When we are not being mindful, unrelated situations can collide, causing bigger turmoil in our lives, affecting innocent bystanders such as our children. While Jasmine was playing with her kids, she decided to read a work email. After reading the unpleasant client message, Jasmine resumed playing with her kids despite feeling troubled and distracted. She told herself she was putting her children first. Suddenly, her six-year-old daughter kicked her four-year-old son, causing him to cry. Already upset, Jasmine instantly screamed at her daughter, causing both children to cry. Jasmine felt terrible after her impulsive reaction and felt like a failure both in her work and mom life. Emotional awareness and utilizing strategies to quell a triggered state can shift your mindset and prevent negative situations from impacting your relationships.

Reactions Reminder

Think about your child's most recent meltdown. Did you reason with them, yell, or demand that they stop? Were you judgmental? Did you attempt to understand their underlying issues and feelings and give them personal space? Write about this experience and then create a calming statement you can say to yourself the next time your child has big feelings. How can you best remind yourself to be compassionate and understanding?

Emotional Awareness

Think about a time when you were upset with your child. Write down all of the emotions that you felt before, during, and after the event. What do you think triggered these feelings? Has this happened before? If so, how did you feel after each time? Understanding the connection between your triggers, feelings, and anger will shift you from a heated reaction to a mindful response in the future.

Deep Belly Breath

Unconsciously, we often take short, shallow breaths, which can induce anxiousness. Deep belly breathing or diaphragmatic breathing lowers stress and curbs emotional reactivity. It also improves sleep, stabilizes blood pressure, and strengthens the immune system.

1. Lie down, placing one hand on your belly and one hand on your chest.

2. Inhale. Fill up your belly with air, noticing your hand on the belly rising. Try not to have the hand on your chest move too much.

3. Exhale. Deflate your belly and notice your hand falling down with the belly.

4. Repeat this pattern for three minutes, then journal how the experience felt.

Mindset Shift

Let's create a diagram of a pattern of thoughts and actions. Recall a time when you spiraled out of control. In the first circle, describe a situation or thought that happened. In the following circles, write down what actions or thoughts happened sequentially until you reach the outcome of the situation: good or bad, resolved or unresolved. Look at each action step and in the rectangle next to it write down how you could have responded differently in that moment.

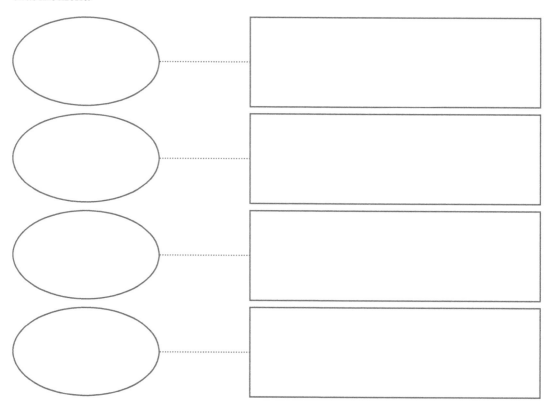

Disarming Triggers

"NO." This tiny word can be a huge trigger. What happened the last time you said no to your child because you were too busy? What happened as a result? Remembering you don't have to say yes to everything, brainstorm some ways you can manage these situations better. What can you say without saying "no"? You might say, "We can read one extra bedtime book," instead of "No. You can't stay up late."

Stop and Take a Time-Out

Sometimes walking away from a heated situation is better than arguing to prove
your point. Creating physical distance interrupts a negativity spiral and refreshes
your mental state. During your next disagreement, either tag out with a partner
or walk away from the situation (if it is safe for your child for you to do so).
While you're separated, try one of the breathing exercises you've learned.
How did this time-out feel? If you returned to the situation,
how did your pause affect your subsequent interactions?

Transference

Think of a time when a seemingly insignificant issue evolved into a big conflict with your partner or child. What events led up to this issue? How did you feel? Could your anger have stemmed from displaced feelings you had about a prior situation or be about a different person altogether?

Detaching from the Past

Past traumas often get internalized and the effects can unfold in your present-day life. To disentangle from a past hardship, write about it below in third person. For example, someone named Sonya would write, "Sonya had a hard time as a teenager . . ." Writing this way detaches you from the situation, making it easier to comprehend how these unresolved issues affect you. The resulting awareness can prevent you from infusing it into future conflicts.

_____

_____

_____

_____

_____

_____

_____

_____

_____

_____

_____

_____

Your Happy Place

The next time you feel upset, close your eyes and go to your happy place. Use your five senses to engage fully with this visualization and allow yourself to be transported to a state of calm and happiness. It can be a place in your everyday life, a previous vacation spot, or something you've seen in pictures.

You Can Do Hard Things

Think of some challenging situations you have lived through. How did you survive those moments? What personal strengths did you utilize or build during those times? It is through struggle that we achieve growth, strength, and resilience. If you were able to do those hard things in the past, what hard things are you facing now that can you handle?

Shift to Acceptance

No matter how hard we try, for the most part we can't change people who don't want to change. Instead, a shift in your viewpoint could be key to improving your relationship. Name some qualities of your child that make up their unique essence. Circle one trait that you find problematic. Write how you can shift your perspective to accept this quality as part of their individuality.

_____

_____

_____

_____

_____

_____

_____

_____

_____

_____

_____

_____

_____

Letting Go

Holding on to past experiences or emotions can weigh heavily on the heart and mind. In this meditation, give yourself permission to let go of the emotions and experiences you no longer need to carry.

1. Close your eyes and notice your breath.

2. Call to mind something you would like to let go of today.

3. Inhale. Breathe in the courage to release and move forward.

4. Exhale. Imagine yourself blowing out that emotion or experience.

5. Repeat this process for five minutes and imagine yourself feeling lighter with each exhalation.

Deflating Tension

Anger can arise from or lead to feelings of rejection, isolation, and sadness. One way to deflate tension during a conflict is to take a mental step back and evaluate the importance of continuing the argument. Think about a recent issue and answer these questions as if you were in the moment: Is this really worth my emotional energy? Will I still care about this issue tomorrow or next week?

_____

_____

_____

_____

_____

_____

_____

_____

_____

_____

_____

De-escalating Through Redirection

Distracting (aka redirecting) your child can work as a de-escalation strategy, especially for younger children and when introduced at the beginning of a tantrum. Recall a recent meltdown. Write out ways you could have redirected your child in a positive way. Then write down what you would have said to your child once everyone calmed down.

Point of View

Getting caught off guard by your child's behavior is an occupational hazard for any parent. But while we can't control everything our child does, we can control our responses. When Monique's eight-year-old daughter, Imogene, called her a bad name in front of her friend, thinking it was funny, Monique was understandably taken aback, as well as feeling disrespected and hurt. Rather than allow those emotions to manifest into anger or admonishment, however, Monique chose to take a beat and calmly (and honestly) explain to Imogene the impact of her words. As the parent, labeling uncomfortable emotions in an escalating situation can help us rid them of their power. And in Monique's case, sharing these emotions had the added benefit of enhancing Imogene's understanding of the consequences of her actions.

I Feel

Naming your emotions separates you from identifying with the feeling or blaming others, for example, saying "I feel angry" instead of "I am angry" or "You made me angry." Voicing "I feel" statements can also help pinpoint what's bubbling within. Think about your last conflict or a recurring situation that makes you upset and write down all of the labeled emotions. What do you feel when you get upset?

_____

_____

_____

_____

_____

_____

_____

_____

_____

_____

_____

Brainstorm Compromises

In the heat of the moment, it can be challenging to come up with fair, alternative solutions to disagreements. Brainstorm compromises in advance that you can offer your child the next time you have a dispute to prevent the situation from spiraling out of control. For example, if siblings are fighting over toys, try something like, "Let's take turns with a timer set for five minutes each."

Problem	Compromise

Communicating Mindfully

Ineffective communication damages relationships
because it hinders understanding and allows connection to deteriorate.
Since mindfulness awakens our awareness of ourselves, our
relationships, and the present moment, we can combine this with
compassion to strengthen our communication with our children.
Mindfulness provides the foundation for strategies such as
active listening and perspective-taking to be productive.

Problem-Solving

Effective communication requires delivering clear, honest messages and open-minded interpretation of the messages by the receiver. But what happens when emotions get in the way and we can't see the other person's viewpoint? While Lee helped her daughter, Mei, with a project, Mei got frustrated about something she could not do. So she shut down and stopped talking. Lee could not understand why her daughter stopped working on the project. Rather than determine the root of the problem, Lee yelled at her daughter, saying, "You have to talk to me so we can finish this!" Mei stormed out of the room, leaving Lee confused and frustrated. Empathy with other people's experiences promotes understanding and enhances communication. As parents, we can model emotional expression and prompt our children with questions to facilitate open communication.

Perspective Taking

Write about a time your child had something bad happen to them or did not get what they wanted. From your child's perspective, write down how they likely perceived the unfairness and why their emotions were justified in their eyes. Now evaluate if their rationale made sense to you. Remember that things you think are simple can be a big deal in the developing mind of a child.

Evaluating Your Communication Skills

Keep track of your interactions with your child over a few days. Make notes in each of these categories to help you reflect and evaluate your communication skills. When looking back at each situation, ask yourself if you listened with an open mind.

EYE CONTACT (LOTS, NONE)					
BODY LANGUAGE (TENSE, RELAXED)					
VOICE LEVEL (CALM, YELLING)					
INTERRUPTIONS (BY YOU OR YOUR CHILD)					
ACKNOWLEDGED FEELINGS (BY YOU OR YOUR CHILD)					
RESOLUTION					

Expressing Emotion

Expressing emotion is difficult at any age. One way to extricate feelings
is to frame their expression in a different way. Sit with your child
while you both draw pictures about a time you each felt sad or mad.
Ask your child to describe the drawing, why they felt that way, and how they
resolved their problem. Then explain your picture to your child,
talking about your feelings and your resolutions.

Healthy Communication Barriers

Often, we parent the same way despite seeing repeated negative results. Write about one flawed interaction with your child. What prevented you from open communication? How could you have approached the situation differently? Did your actions stem from your own upbringing?

_____

_____

_____

_____

_____

_____

_____

_____

_____

_____

_____

_____

Mindful Listening

Recall a time your child had a problem when, rather than listening to their story, you immediately jumped to your own conclusions and judgments. Why do you think you stopped listening? What feelings did you have? Imagine you returned to this moment mindfully listening instead. Write how this would have changed your interaction.

Family Values

It's easier for a family to adhere to expectations when they are clear to everyone. Make a list of all the family values that you and your partner feel are important. Narrow them down to a list of six to eight options and ask your child or children to help pick your family's final four. This conversation will empower them to share what they find important and incentivize them to be accountable to the values they chose.

Consistency Is Key

Kids need consistency to understand and abide by rules. When you flip-flop, it is confusing for them and mixes up their boundaries and expectations. Reflect on recent conflicts. Were your instructions, rules, and consequences clear and consistent? Did you and your partner give inconsistent messaging to your child? If you changed your mind on an issue, did you explain it? How could you make these messages clearer?

What Do I Need?

Parents can fail to recognize and convey their own needs, which leads to frustration and misdirected anger. Describe a moment when you struggled with your child. Why did you feel this way? What were your needs in that moment (safety, love, respect) that weren't being met? Write how you could have expressed yourself more effectively in that scenario.

I Understand

Navigating a child's public or private tantrums is something parents inevitably experience. How we respond in the heat of the moment informs our children how they should respond to challenges in their own lives. While dining at a restaurant, Diego's five-year-old son, Paulo, excitedly waited for his favorite dessert only to learn it was sold out. Paulo burst into a crying fit. Diego was embarrassed and wanted to run out of the restaurant. Instead, he closed his eyes, visualized his happy place, and took some deep breaths. Upon calming down, Diego looked Paulo in the eyes and said, "I'm sorry about the brownie. I understand you feel frustrated and upset." When parents pause and reset their mindset, the resulting clarity allows for validation of your child's feelings.

Modeling Patience

Parents model good and bad behavior for their children. Demonstrating patience during an argument informs your child how to navigate confrontations calmly and respectfully without yelling. Write about a time you were not patient with your child. How did this feel and get resolved? How could you have modeled patience to your child?

_____

_____

_____

_____

_____

_____

_____

_____

_____

_____

_____

_____

_____

Expressing Empathy

Recall an unmet expectation your child experienced. How did your child react? How did you react to your child's response? Write down an alternative response that expresses your empathy or understanding of their feelings in a nonjudgmental way.

Validation

The next time you feel the urge to yell, try to acknowledge your child's point of view. This validates their feelings and conveys their importance to you. Validating doesn't mean you necessarily agree, it just gives your child a safe space to be heard. Try the statements below and then journal about your experience.

· Your feelings make sense.
· I see that you are feeling . . .
· What I hear you saying is . . .
· I'm sorry I didn't understand that you were feeling . . .
· How can I support you?

_____

_____

_____

_____

Resolving Conflict

Apologies aren't easy at any age because they require vulnerability and acceptance of wrongdoing. However, they're part of healthy and productive conflict resolution and communication. Think about a conflict your child had that was not resolved well. Write the language you could have coached your child to say that includes:

Remorse and request for forgiveness: "I'm sorry."

_____

_____

_____

Acknowledgment/ownership: "I take responsibility for . . ."

_____

_____

_____

Solution: "Why don't we try to . . ."

_____

_____

_____

Framing Messages

Being mindful of your words can result in healthier communication with your children. The words you say can affect your child's self-image and outlook. Write down statements you've said to your child that could be seen as negative and reframe them in a positive way. "Eating your veggies makes you healthy and strong" is a better alternative to "Good boys eat their vegetables."

Infinity Hugging Breath

The next time your child cries, try this technique to calm you and your child.

1. At the onset of crying, scoop your child into a hug.

2. While hugging your child, begin the infinity breath: breathe in slowly and without pausing, flow your inhalation into your exhalation. Do not ask your child to join you in the breath.

3. Repeat and stay present by witnessing the rise and fall of your body as you inhale and exhale.

4. Once your child stops crying and you feel calm, ask your child to take a deep breath then begin a dialogue about your child's emotions and needs.

Consciously Connecting

In previous sections, you awakened your connection to
yourself through acts of mindfulness fueled by courage, vulnerability,
and honesty. This section challenges you and your child to embrace
awareness and deepen your connection with one another.
By learning new habits, you'll encourage intention and
nurture positivity and independence.

Helicopter Parenting

As parents, we want the best for our children, but this sometimes translates into exerting control, which oversteps boundaries and stifles independence and creativity. Kiara's five-year-old son, Houston, was working on a craft for a Father's Day gift. Kiara laid out all of the materials and told her son to use anything he wanted. Yet, each time Houston did something, Kiara interjected and told him to do something else or added things to the craft herself. No longer having fun, Houston went to play with his toys leaving Kiara to finish the project. She felt guilty. Why did she keep struggling with how to teach her son new things? Being mindful of our children's individuality allows us to encourage and nurture their growth in a positive way.

Go with the Flow

When was the last time that you let go of control of a situation with your child and just experienced the moment as it happened? How did it feel to be present and go with the flow? Was it unnerving, exciting, stressful? Why? What was your child's experience and reaction?

Let Go to Grow

Growth in any capacity is tough, it takes courage to step out of the old and into the new. Growth is fueled by love and a dedication for improvement. What does parental growth look like for you? What habits do you need to let go of to grow for yourself and your family? What benefits will come from making this space?

Nurturing Independence

Allow your child's individuality to blossom. Provide them the opportunity and gift of exploring the world uninhibited by expectations. You can do this today by setting up a brand-new activity for your child and then standing back and being mindful of how they explore this new task. Notice their expressions, words, and body language. Afterward, have a discussion about their experience finding out what they liked, disliked, and found surprising.

Creating Family Boundaries

Boundaries are critical to protecting one's wellness. They help us define personal limits and ensure safety. Setting and abiding to boundaries in relationships also encourages and enriches mutual respect and trust. What are the boundaries you need for yourself and for your family? Write down in the table what boundaries your child and partner have as individuals. Circle the boundaries that are being met and note ones that need work.

MY BOUNDARIES	FAMILY BOUNDARIES	CHILD BOUNDARIES	PARTNER BOUNDARIES
E.g., alone time	E.g., honesty		

Working Together

Think about a problem your child was having, either with you or elsewhere, that you solved for them. How could you have encouraged your child to work with you to formulate solutions? Role-playing conversations is a great way to work together when your child has arguments with friends. Try this teamwork strategy with your child and journal about the outcome. Collaboration encourages respect and understanding.

_____

_____

_____

_____

_____

_____

_____

_____

_____

_____

_____

_____

_____

Cell Phone Lockdown

Twenty minutes of uninterrupted, full-focused fun with your child can be more rewarding than two hours of distracted time. Set a timer on your phone for 20 minutes and walk away from it. Spend the time engaging with your child in whatever they're spontaneously doing. Be mindful of everything that is happening in the present moment. How did you and your child respond to this focused time together? Were you able to stay present? How did you deal with distractions?

Making Time to Connect

What moments of the day is your child more open to sharing their feelings? Pay attention to patterns, making note of them below. When they open up, drop everything you can and actively listen with an open heart and mind. How do you think it makes your child feel to be heard? What are you learning? What do you hope to learn?

Positive Parenting

Emotional nourishment is a key factor in positive parenting. Prior to altering behavior, you need to connect with your child. Think about your own inner child, the one we carry from our past that can still affect us today. How would you connect to your inner child in a positive manner? Write out what you'd want to hear. Now write some affirming statements you can say to your child.

_____

_____

_____

_____

_____

_____

_____

_____

_____

_____

Practicing Encouragement

Write about a time your child approached you happily and proudly with something that could be construed as a misstep or something not so great (for example, when "making a craft" can seem like "making a mess"). How did you respond? Why? Were there expectations, boundaries, or triggers that affected your response? How could you have responded in a way that encouraged your child's independence, creativity, and spirit?

_____

_____

_____

_____

_____

_____

_____

_____

_____

_____

_____

_____

Reflections on Connections

What are your top three memories from childhood? What do you hope your child will remember about their childhood? Write a letter to your child to read when they're your current age that includes reflections of how you consciously connected together. Identifying what's important to you will give you mindful guidance of how to navigate parenthood.

_____

_____

_____

_____

_____

_____

_____

_____

_____

_____

_____

_____

_____

_____

_____

Nature Walk

Exploring nature with your child is a great introduction to mindfulness. Ask your child to make a list of things to find during your walk (flowers, birds, rocks, animals). While walking, find things on your list and encourage your child to touch, smell, or listen to things. Pause to appreciate beauty. Revel in the peace and joy that it sparks within. Ask your child to describe what they like about each item. Mindful nature walks can boost your immune system and increase calm and happiness within.

Modeling Resilience

The ability to recover from challenges improves our confidence and bravery. Our response also informs our children how to be resilient. Write an explanation to your kids of a challenging situation you experienced. Include your thoughts, feelings, and actions of dealing with the situation in a resilient way.

_____

_____

_____

_____

_____

_____

_____

_____

_____

_____

_____

Cultivating Consciousness

Strengthening your bond with your child requires intentional action. There is often an internal battle of how we instinctively react to our child versus how we want to respond to them. Check in with your interactions for a few days to keep focused on cultivating conscious connections.

DATE	WAS I PRESENT TODAY?	IN WHAT WAY(S) DID I CONNECT WITH MY CHILD?	WHAT'S ONE WAY I CAN IMPROVE OUR CONNECTION TOMORROW?

Sharing Love

For each family member, ask your child to share things they love most
about this person. Write it on separate notes, then ask your child to decorate it.
Now share with your child what you love most about them, putting it on a note.
Hand them the note as you make eye contact and say, "I love you," giving them
a hug. Ask your child to give their notes to each family member,
in the same way. This exercise builds awareness and kindness and
promotes the mind-body connection of social bonding.

Cultivating Gratitude, Joy, and Peace

Gratitude has a multitude of benefits beyond just an appreciation for the good things in life. Cultivating gratitude is a wonderful tool for shifting mindset, enhancing relationships, improving health, and overcoming adversity. Gratitude ultimately sparks joy and evokes peace within.

Taking Joy for Granted

When life gets busy, it can feel hard to slow down. It becomes easy to take life's joys for granted. While Marina worked, her mom took care of her kids. Every night Marina came home from work and hastily expressed thanks to her mom but felt too exhausted to talk. After her mom passed away suddenly, Marina finally noticed little things she took for granted that her mom always did, such as tidying up the kids' rooms and stocking their favorite treats in the kitchen. Mindful of this missed opportunity, Marina committed to being more appreciative of her loved ones. Consciously connecting to ourselves and others cultivates gratitude and joy and elevates our relationships.

Thank-You Letter

When reflecting on the important things in life, we often realize it isn't the possessions, but rather the people, that are most important. During times of loss, people often regret not sharing sentiments of love and appreciation with loved ones who have passed. Take this opportunity to write and give a letter to someone important to you, sharing your gratitude and special memories.

_____

_____

_____

_____

_____

_____

_____

_____

_____

_____

_____

_____

_____

Appreciate Yourself

Before sharing gratitude and joy with others, take a moment to love yourself first. Write down all the things you appreciate about yourself, from the past to the present, no matter how big or small. It can be qualities about yourself, how you interact with others, or things you achieved.

_____

_____

_____

_____

_____

_____

_____

_____

_____

_____

_____

Loving-Kindness

Loving-kindness or "Metta" meditation is a practice where we extend
goodwill and compassion first to ourselves, so we can then share it with others.
Say the following phrases to yourself, hand over heart,
slowly breathing in and out with each phrase:

May I be happy.
May I be healthy.
May I be safe.
May I live with peace and joy.

Now envision someone you love and say to them, "May you be happy."
Repeat this for the rest of the phrases.
Follow this pattern when thinking about someone with whom you
have a conflict. End by directing the phrases to the world.

Joyful Balance

Make each day fulfilling by balancing between things that bring joy with the tedious things in life. Identify what brings you happiness. If you had all the time and money in the world, what are the things that you would choose to do right now? How can you incorporate more time in your day or week to include a tiny bit of this passion to balance out the daily drudgery?

Glass Half Full

Looking at life through a lens of abundance versus scarcity creates feelings of gratitude, peace, and joy. Shift your mindset to focus on the goodness of life versus what you lack. Write down all the scarcity thoughts you have and next to it write down a version of abundance.

SCARCITY STATEMENT	ABUNDANCE STATEMENT
I wish I was more patient with the kids.	I am thankful I'm taking the time to learn to be more patient with my kids.

Bedtime Breathing

Brains are still developing during childhood, so it's advantageous to teach your child mindfulness and calming strategies during this time.
Bedtime is a productive teaching time, because there are minimal distractions. Practice this method of bedtime breathing to help your child manage their emotions and peacefully settle into sleep:

1. Ask your child to count to four while you inhale through your nose, and count to four as you exhale.

2. Now ask your child to breathe in and out while you count to four each time.

3. Together, follow the same breathing pattern while keeping count on your fingers.

Peace Out

Tapping into our inner peace leads to awakened experiences. What would a peaceful day look like to you? What prevents you from achieving this vision and what steps can you take to make at least one peaceful moment happen each day? How do you think your child's version of peace compares? How do you encourage peace and calm in your family?

Words Matter

Reframe the way you look at life's tasks through the viewpoint of gratitude. One simple word can change our perspective on life and pivot our minds to positivity. For example, you might think, "I *get* to do this," rather than "I *have* to do this." What are some things you *feel* you have to do? Rewrite those tasks and obligations below by saying, "I *get to . . .*"

I HAVE TO . . .	I GET TO . . .

Life Is Better

Often it takes perspective to see what's good in your life, especially if you're making moves toward positive change. Pretend that you are looking down at your life and observe the goodness. How is your life better because you are a parent? Complete this statement about the many aspects of your life that are good or have improved: "Life is better because ..."

Relive Joy

If you could relive one day in your life, what would it be and why? Are there any ways that you could replicate the important parts of this joyousness even in little ways? For example, if you are married, you can relive the joy of your wedding by going out with your spouse and discussing other happy moments together. Describe the day you'd like to relive here and write down ways you can recapture the feeling of that experience:

Gratitude of the Day

Model the appreciation of life and share the benefits of gratitude with your family. Pick a time when your family is all together, such as a family dinner. Share some of the benefits you have experienced as a result of being more thankful. Say how often you'd like your family's new gratitude practice to happen. Take turns sharing one gratitude for your day and acknowledge each person's gratitude in a positive and encouraging way.

Pay It Forward

An active way to harness joy within yourself is to bring happiness to others. Write down one thing you can do each day this week to make someone happy. It can be sharing a smile, sending an appreciative text, or buying a gift. After each experience, write down the person's reaction, how you felt in that moment of giving, and the impact of your gestures.

One Year Later

Envision your life a year from now. How did you incorporate the techniques from this mindfulness journey into your life and your parent-child relationship? How did you feel during your moments of mindfulness? How did this focused awareness impact your life and your family?

_____

_____

_____

_____

_____

_____

_____

_____

_____

_____

_____

_____

_____

Setting Intentions Meditation

Intentions are the purpose or motivation behind the actions you take to achieve a goal. As we conclude this journal, set an intention to remind yourself to infuse mindfulness in your life and parenting.

1. Close your eyes. Witness your breath.

2. Call to mind your intention for continuing your journey of growth and awareness.

3. With every breath you take, breathe in your intention and allow it to take root within.

4. Use your intention as the mantra you repeat to keep you anchored in the present moment.

5. After your meditation, write down your intention as a reminder for your continued mindfulness practice.

Resources

Apps

Breathwork. Breathing exercises to help you decrease anxiety and improve energy and focus.

Happify. Activities and games to reduce anxiety and stress.

Podcasts

McManne, Robbin. *Parenting our Future.* Podcast audio.

Harvey, Cara. *Purpose Driven Mom Show.* Podcast audio.

Atluri, Josephine. *Responding to Life: Talking Health, Fertility, and Parenthood.* Podcast audio.

Social Media

Mindful Parenting with Josephine Atluri Facebook Group. Connect with other parents looking to infuse mindfulness into their daily parenting.

Josephine Atluri Meditation channel. Try out video meditations on YouTube made with the beginner in mind.

Websites

Mindful Parenting Class

MindfulParentClass.com

Companion class to this journal with video meditations and bonus material.

Positive Psychology

PositivePsychology.com/blog

Articles on gratitude, mindfulness, compassion, and mindset.

Self-compassion

Neff, Kristin. *Self-Compassion.org.*

References

Chödrön, Pema. *When Things Fall Apart: Heart Advice for Difficult Times*. Boulder, Colorado: Shambhala Publications, Inc, 1997.

Davidji. *Destressifying: The Real-World Guide to Personal Empowerment, Lasting Fulfillment, and Peace of Mind*. New York: Hay House, Inc., 2015.

Dweck, Carol S. *Mindset: The New Psychology of Success*. New York: Ballantine Books, 2006.

Schwartz, Suzanne Yalof, with Debra Goldstein. *Unplug: A Simple Guide to Meditation for Busy Skeptics and Modern Soul Seekers*. New York: Harmony Books, 2017.

Simon, Tami. *The Self-Acceptance Project: How to be Kind and Compassionate Toward Yourself in Any Situation*. Boulder, Colorado: Sounds True, 2016.

Tolle, Eckhart. *The Power of Now: A Guide to Spiritual Enlightenment*. Novato, California: New World Library, 1999/2004.

Acknowledgments

Thank you for this amazing opportunity, Callisto Media!

A huge thank-you to my husband, Pramod, for always believing in and supporting me as I chased my dreams. Without you, none of this is possible. I am grateful to be your partner and walk this life with you.

Thank you to my parents, Joe and Carol, and my in-laws, Rajendra and Indira, for your unyielding support and encouragement. You are all shining examples of sacrifice and dedication in the spirit of unconditional and selfless love.

I am grateful for the help along my mindfulness journey provided by PIVOT, Farita Reyes Social Media, Light Years Ahead PR, Kristen Mann Design, Dieter Jacobs P.A., Allysa Sing, The Network Studios, Patty, Yetunde, Suze Yalof Schwartz, and davidji.

To my darling children, Jaiden, Malena, Mateo, Deion, and Dante, thank you for being my why. You fuel my passion to live mindfully and help others so that I can be a model of a life lived with purpose. Remember to take a deep breath when things get tough and never forget you are capable of anything. With hard work and dedication, you can make your dreams a reality. I love you all.

About the Author

Josephine Atluri is an expert in meditation and mindfulness who has helped thousands of people overcome adversity to find joy. A University of Chicago graduate, Josephine spent many years consulting for Fortune 500 companies and private clients. Pursuing her passion for total wellness, she became certified as a meditation teacher through Unplug Meditation. Josephine combines her business background with her meditation training to teach corporate mindfulness sessions. Her experience creating her modern-day family of five children via in vitro fertilization, international adoption, and surrogacy inspires her work as a highly-sought-after fertility and parenting mindfulness coach.

Josephine hosts a popular podcast, *Responding to Life: Talking Health, Fertility, and Parenthood*, where she interviews guests on their inspiring responses to life's challenges. Her parenting mindfulness expertise and fertility advocacy work has been featured in Motherly, MindBodyGreen, The Bump, *Prevention Magazine*, Well+Good, and *Woman's Day*. Josephine lives with her husband, five children, and cockapoo in what she likes to call her "Casa de Calm con Chaos" in Los Angeles, California.

CPSIA information can be obtained
at www.ICGtesting.com
Printed in the USA
BVHW051807231021
619536BV00001B/2

9 781648 764691